Published by Creative Education
123 South Broad Street, Mankato, Minnesota 56001
Creative Education is an imprint of The Creative Company

Art direction by Rita Marshall
Production design by The Design Lab

Photographs by Artemis Images (ATD Group, Inc.), Corbis (Hulton-Deutsch, George Hall,
Underwood & Underwood), Defense Visual Information Center, Gregory Fischer,
Richard Gross, Derk R. Kuyper, Sally McCrae Kuyper, North Wind Picture Archives,
Otto G. Richter Library (Archives & Special Collections, University of Miami, Coral Gables,
Florida), Bonnie Sue Rauch, Reuters (Doug Wilson), D. Jeanene Tiner, John Wilson

Copyright © 2004 Creative Education.
International copyrights reserved in all countries.
No part of this book may be reproduced in any form
without written permission from the publisher.
Printed in the United States of America.

Library of Congress Cataloging-in-Publication Data

Tiner, John Hudson, 1944–
Airplanes / by John Hudson Tiner.
p. cm. — (Let's investigate)
Summary: An introduction to the history of flight and to
specific airplanes of the past, present, and future.
ISBN 1-58341-258-1
1. Aeronautics—Juvenile literature. 2. Airplanes—Juvenile literature.
[1. Airplanes. 2. Aeronautics.] I. Title. II. Series.
TL546 .T59   2003
629.133'34—dc21   2002031496

First edition

2 4 6 8 9 7 5 3 1

AIRPLANES

JOHN HUDSON TINER

DISCARD

Creative Education

...nton Area Schools
...2 North Main Street
...ranton, WI 54436

AIRPLANE
STORY

In a story in Greek mythology, a man named Icarus fashioned wings out of feathers and wax. But when he flew too close to the sun, the wax melted and he fell into the sea.

4

Above, a man trying to fly like a bird
Right, one of the first experimental planes

People have long dreamed of quick and easy transportation over land, on water, and through the air. Thousands of years ago, ancient inventors built wheeled carriages to travel over the ground. People by the sea designed boats to sail mighty rivers and the vast oceans. But soaring through the air like birds remained a dream until brave sky pioneers learned to fly.

AIRPLANE

FAILURE

Early aircraft builders tried to use steam engines to create thrust, or forward motion. Although powerful, steam engines were too heavy to allow airplanes to get off the ground.

AIRPLANE
WINGS

Many early aircraft were biplanes. They had two sets of wings, one over the other, to increase lift (the force that makes a plane rise). Many crop-dusting planes are biplanes because they need to be able to turn and climb quickly.

Otto Lilienthal in flight under one of his gliders

THE FIRST FLYERS

For a long time, attempting flight was a very dangerous business. In 1891, a German **engineer** named Otto Lilienthal began experimenting with human-carrying **gliders**. Instead of flapping wings like a bird, he launched himself into the wind from a 50-foot (15 m) hill. Once airborne, he changed direction by shifting his body around and swinging his legs. Lilienthal made more than 2,000 flights. But on August 8, 1896, a gust of wind upset his

glider. Lilienthal could not regain control. He crashed to the ground and died.

Across the ocean, in Dayton, Ohio, Wilbur Wright and his younger brother, Orville, designed and sold bicycles. The Wright brothers read of the tragic death of Lilienthal, and their thoughts turned to building an airplane that the pilot could control even in windy conditions.

AIRPLANE
SKETCHES

In the late 1400s, Leonardo da Vinci, the Italian artist who painted the Mona Lisa, *watched birds to learn about flight and sketched flying machines with flapping wings.*

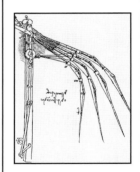

Above, a sketch by Leonardo da Vinci Left, Wilbur (top) and Orville (bottom) Wright

AIRPLANE
EXPENSE

American scientist Simon Langley spent $100,000 building three experimental airplanes, but all crashed. He gave up just 10 days before the Wrights made the first flight.

The Wrights' airplane was a biplane with a simple skeletal structure

O rville observed buzzards through binoculars. He saw that the large birds twisted feathers at the tips of their wings to control their gliding flights. The Wrights built a glider that was big enough for a person but could be flown from the ground as a kite. Twisted wing tips kept the glider balanced.

The Wrights then traveled by train to North Carolina. A site near the town of Kitty Hawk offered steady winds that were perfect for flight attempts. There, the young inventors proved that they could

effectively control their glider in flight. The final obstacle they faced was finding a source of power besides the wind to propel their aircraft. They returned home and built a lightweight gasoline engine. The water-cooled, **internal combustion engine** developed about 12 **horsepower**.

AIRPLANE
INDICATOR

Most small airports have a windsock—a tube of lightweight fabric that swings around to show which direction the wind is blowing.

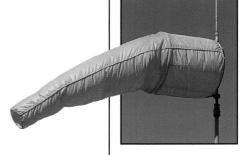

Above, windsocks are simple but helpful aviation aids

AIRPLANE
CHANCE

Wilbur and Orville Wright tossed a coin to decide who would fly first. Wilbur won, but he crashed. Three days later (December 17, 1903), after making repairs, it was Orville's turn. He succeeded.

Above, a monument at Kitty Hawk Right, the Flyer aloft in France in 1908

The next year, the Wrights returned to Kitty Hawk. On December 17, 1903, they made the first successful flight in a full-sized airplane. Orville piloted their plane, the *Flyer*, a distance of 120 feet (37 m) in 12 seconds. Although it was a short flight, it was flight nonetheless, and the Wright brothers secured an honored place in aviation history.

The original Wright brothers airplane, the Flyer, *and Lindbergh's* Spirit of St. Louis *are on display at the National Air and Space Museum in Washington, D.C.*

11

CONTROL, LIFT, AND THRUST

The Wright brothers' most important flight breakthrough was learning how to control airplanes and keep them balanced in flight. To take off, change direction, and land, a pilot must be skilled at manipulating a plane's controls. An airplane has three main control surfaces: elevators, ailerons, and the rudder. Cables connect these moveable surfaces to the control wheel or stick that the pilot holds to fly the plane.

Above, a Spirit of St. Louis *replica Left, Wilbur Wright at the controls*

AIRPLANE

ENGINE

A jet engine compresses air with spinning blades and mixes in fuel. When the fuel ignites, it escapes through a nozzle to produce the force that propels the airplane.

12

Elevators are part of the horizontal stabilizer, the structure that looks like a small wing at the back of the plane. When the pilot pulls back on the stick, the elevators on the tail rise. The raised elevators catch the wind, forcing the tail down and the nose of the plane up. Pushing forward on the stick causes the nose to pitch down.

Elevators help to control the degree of a plane's ascent or descent

Pilots reduce or increase engine power to change altitude. Going faster increases lift, and the airplane rises. A pilot can descend slowly by reducing power.

13

Ailerons are moveable surfaces on the back edge of the main wings. Pushing the stick to the left raises the left aileron and lowers the right aileron. Air catches the ailerons and causes the left wing to dip and the right wing to rise. Pushing the stick to the right has the opposite effect.

Above, skilled pilots can put on spectacular aerial shows
Left, ailerons

AIRPLANE
STREAMS

Jet pilots take advantage of fast-flowing, high-altitude winds known as jet streams to increase speed and fly between cities faster.

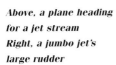

Above, a plane heading for a jet stream Right, a jumbo jet's large rudder

The rudder is part of the vertical stabilizer—an upright fin—on the tail of an airplane. It turns the plane left or right. While turning with the rudder, the pilot also banks the plane by moving the ailerons. This makes the airplane turn smoothly.

AIRPLANE

LIFT

The wings of a small airplane produce about 72 pounds (33 kg) of lift per square foot (929 sq cm) of its surface, or about 3,000 pounds (1,364 kg) of lift over its entire surface.

AIRPLANE

PHYSICS

You can see lift in action by holding a strip of paper under your lower lip and blowing. The paper rises because fast-moving air exerts less pressure than the air under the paper.

Air pressure under wings can keep aloft even a plane weighing many tons

Airplanes need lift to overcome gravity and become airborne. A wing produces lift because of its shape. The bottom surface is flat, and the upper surface is rounded. Air passing across the wing exerts less pressure on the top than on the bottom. The difference in air pressure causes the wing to rise.

AIRPLANE
PROPELLER

The Wrights' Flyer had two propellers that the brothers carved out of wood. The engine turned the propellers with bicycle chains.

Above, early airplanes used wooden propellers Right, some modern planes still feature propellers

Thrust is the force that propels an airplane through the air. Birds push themselves through the air by flapping their wings. Birds can fly because they have powerful muscles and lightweight bodies. In airplanes, propellers or jet engines provide thrust.

Today, a large pas-
senger jet such as a
Boeing 747 is near-
ly 1,000 different
dials and instru-
ments in the cockpit.

An airplane's **cockpit** has five instruments in particular that the pilot
watches closely. An altimeter tells the pilot the altitude, or height above
the ground. A compass shows the direction the airplane is headed. A
turn and bank indicator displays whether or not the wings are level and whether
the plane is turning. An air speed indicator reports the plane's speed. And the fuel
gauge displays how much gasoline remains in the fuel tank.

*Above, a cockpit and
its many gauges
Left, four of a plane's
five key instruments*

AIRPLANE
LUCK

During Louis Blériot's crossing of the English Channel, his 25-horsepower, air-cooled engine overheated, and the plane threatened to crash. Luckily, a passing rainstorm cooled the engine so he could continue.

AIRPLANE
HISTORY

Alberto Santos-Dumont, a wealthy businessman from Brazil, became the first person to fly in Europe. In 1906, he flew his plane, which looked like a box kite, over Paris.

Louis Blériot posing with his airplane after his historic flight in 1909

AVIATION TAKES OFF

In 1909, French pilot Louis Blériot crossed the English Channel in an airplane. His 23-mile (37 km) journey carried him from his takeoff near Calais, France, to a landing in a meadow just beyond the white cliffs of Dover, England. The 37-minute flight proved that oceans need not be a barrier to air travel.

Blériot landed in a meadow because very few airports had been built. Airplane builders, such as American Glenn Curtiss, realized that if a plane could land on water, then rivers, lakes, and harbors could serve as convenient runways. In 1911, Curtiss developed **pontoons** as an alternative to wheeled landing gear, which allowed his airplanes to land on water.

AIRPLANE
INVENTOR

Alexander Graham Bell, the inventor of the telephone, was an avid aviation pioneer. He built large kites to test his ideas, and he helped Glenn Curtiss develop pontoon aircraft.

Above, Alexander Graham Bell
Left, an airplane with pontoons

AIRPLANE
VERSATILITY

An amphibious aircraft can land on water and then taxi, or roll, onto land. Under the pontoons are small wheels that allow the plane to roll across solid surfaces.

AIRPLANE
SERVICE

The American company United Airlines hired the first passenger airplane flight attendants, called stewardesses, in 1930. They were all nurses, all women, and all under 25 years of age.

Flying boats expanded airplanes' capabilities in the early 20th century

I n 1912, Curtiss built the first flying boat, a plane with a boat-like hull that could float on water. One of his flying boats ran the world's first regular passenger service. The historic route opened in 1914 and flew between the Florida cities of St. Petersburg and Tampa. The **seaplane** carried one passenger at a time across Tampa Bay, covering the 21-mile (34 km) distance in 23 minutes.

People felt safe traveling in flying boats on long trips across the ocean. In the event that the engines failed, the airplane could land on the water. The most famous of the flying boats were Pan America Airline's Clippers, which were built in the 1930s. A Clipper had a kitchen, a dining room, sleeping berths for 40 passengers—and an anchor.

AIRPLANE
TRAGEDY

In 1932, Amelia Earhart became the first woman to fly solo across the Atlantic. Later, she began an around-the-world flight, but her plane disappeared over the Pacific. She was never seen again.

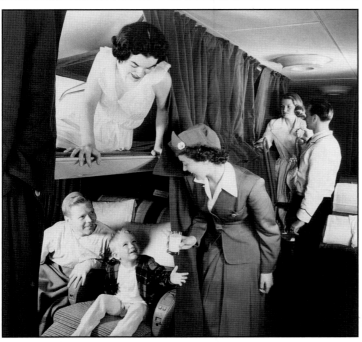

Above, Amelia Earhart
Left, a Clipper outside (top) and inside (bottom)

AIRPLANE
LUNCH

Charles Lindbergh took two canteens of water, a bag of sandwiches, and a hard-boiled egg on his trans-Atlantic flight.

AIRPLANE
DANGER

Before Lindbergh took off, Richard Byrd and other famous pilots had already tried to cross the Atlantic Ocean. Their planes either crashed on takeoff or disappeared over the stormy Atlantic.

Charles Lindbergh earned worldwide fame with his record-setting flight

Interest in flying took a great leap forward in 1927. That was the year that Charles A. Lindbergh became the most famous flyer in history. Lindbergh began his aviation career transporting mail between St. Louis and Chicago. He read about a $25,000 prize being offered to the first pilot to make a nonstop flight from New York City to Paris, France. The 25-year-old Lindbergh became determined to collect that prize. Businessmen in St. Louis loaned Lindbergh the money to buy an airplane, which he named the *Spirit of St. Louis*. The plane had only one seat for the solo flight, and newspapers called Lindbergh the "Lone Eagle."

Early on the morning of May 20, 1927, the *Spirit of St. Louis* began to roll down muddy Roosevelt Field outside New York City. The airplane was heavy with gasoline, and the wheels sank into the mud. As the plane gained speed, the wheels skipped once, twice, and then pulled free. Thirty-three hours and 39 minutes later, Lindbergh's airplane cut through the darkness and bounced to a stop at LaBourget Field near Paris. The flight made Lindbergh a hero, and the public accepted aviation with confidence for the first time.

AIRPLANE
FUEL

Lindbergh's Spirit of St. Louis *carried 450 gallons (1,703 l) of fuel. One of the fuel tanks blocked his forward view, so he used a periscope to see in front of him.*

The Spirit of St. Louis soaring near the Eiffel Tower in Paris, France

AIRPLANE
B O O M

A sonic boom is the loud sound that occurs when an airplane flies faster than the speed of sound. It is not a single bang but a continuous noise that follows along behind the plane.

AIRPLANE
MINI-BOOM

The crack of a whip is a tiny sonic boom. The whip pops back so quickly that the tip exceeds the speed of sound.

Sleek and compact, the Bell X-1 set a new benchmark in high-speed travel

FASTER THAN SOUND

In the 1940s, engineers developed airplanes powered by jet engines. Jet airplanes flew higher and faster than propeller-driven aircraft. But this development wasn't without its problems. Planes that approached the speed of sound shook violently. Pilots often lost control, and sometimes planes broke apart. Engineers called this problem the **sound barrier** because they thought a plane could not go faster than sound. (The speed of sound changes depending on the altitude and temperature. High in the air, the speed of sound is about 660 miles (1,062 km) per hour.)

The United States government built an experimental aircraft called the *Bell X-1* to test whether a plane could indeed fly

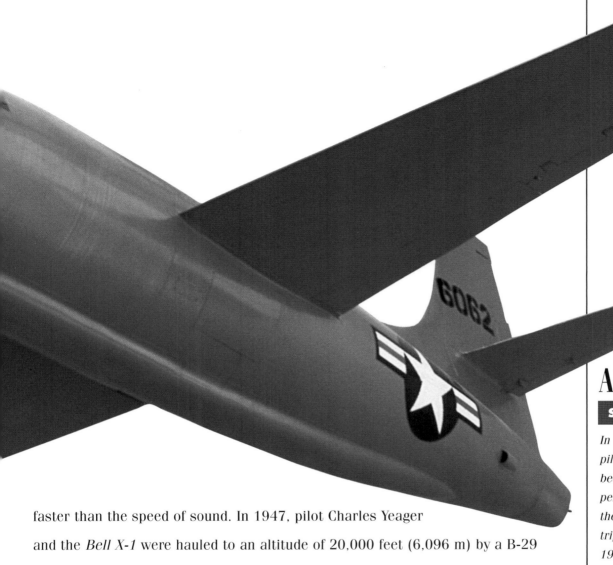

faster than the speed of sound. In 1947, pilot Charles Yeager and the *Bell X-1* were hauled to an altitude of 20,000 feet (6,096 m) by a B-29 bomber aircraft. The airplane was released, and Yeager ignited the **rocket engine**. The *Bell X-1* shot up to 40,000 feet (12,192 m) and broke the sound barrier, making Yeager the first human being to travel faster than the speed of sound.

AIRPLANE
SOLITUDE

In 1933, American pilot Wiley Post became the first person to fly around the world solo. The trip took 7 days and 19 hours.

AIRPLANE
GIANT

The huge seaplane Spruce Goose *was made almost entirely of wood and had a wingspan of 319 feet (97 m). It flew only once—a short test flight in 1947.*

The Comet **was more than three times faster than Lindbergh's** Spirit **of St. Louis**

Two years later, the first jet **airliner** was built in England. It was called the *Comet* and flew passengers from London to South Africa at a speed of near-ly 500 miles (805 km) per hour. In 1969, British and French companies worked together to build the first **supersonic** passenger airplane. The Concorde flew at twice the speed of sound—about 1,450 miles (2,334 km) per hour—and could cross the Atlantic Ocean in three and a half hours.

AIRPLANE
JUMP

The first parachute jump from an airplane was made in St. Louis, Missouri, in 1912 by Captain Albert Berry of the United States Army.

SPECIAL-PURPOSE AIRCRAFT

There are many types of airplanes in the world today, each built for one special function. A crop duster is a plane used on farms. It seeds fields with winter wheat or other crops when the ground is too wet for tractors. In the spring, it drops fertilizer and later spreads weed killers and insecticides. A crop duster turns quickly, flies close to the ground, and carries heavy loads.

Above, a parachutist Left, a crop duster spreading insecticides

AIRPLANE

LONGEVITY

The McDonald Douglas DC-3 was a propeller-driven aircraft that carried 21 passengers. First flown in 1933, some DC-3s were still in the air 65 years later.

Above, a DC-3
Right, this plane has fabric composite wings and metal ailerons

Some planes are designed to carry only a few passengers, such as traveling businessmen, at high speeds. Instead of metal, some of these aircraft are constructed of lightweight **composite materials** such as carbon fibers woven together and strengthened with special glue. Such light planes can fly faster than heavier ones.

In 1979, Bryan Allen pedaled the Gossamer Albatross across the English Channel. The 86-pound (39 kg) plane was made of plastic, and Allen's muscles were its only source of power.

29

An **ultralight** is as small as a hang glider but has a seat and an engine. **Jumbo jets** carry hundreds of passengers at nearly the speed of sound. Some airplanes are capable of taking off from short runways, such as fighter jets that are launched from the short decks of aircraft carriers. Still other aircraft can tilt their engines so they can land like helicopters.

Ultralights offer the freedom of flight in a vehicle the size of a car

AIRPLANE
OPERATION

NASA's space shuttles fly as airplanes within Earth's atmosphere, as spacecraft while in orbit, and as gliders with the engines turned off when they return to Earth.

AIRPLANE
ALTITUDE

A pilot who flies higher than 50 miles (80 km) is considered an astronaut. At that altitude, the aircraft is above most of the atmosphere, and stars become visible even during the day.

With airplanes, even the other side of the world doesn't seem so far away

The history of flight has been filled with obstacles that seemed to defy solutions. Yet brave pilots and skilled aircraft engineers have overcome virtually all challenges. Today, engineers are designing aircraft that will be faster, quieter, and generate less pollution than the planes of today. They are also designing simple planes that will be inexpensive and easy to fly. Who knows? Perhaps one day people will fly personal planes instead of driving cars!

Glossary

An **airliner** is an aircraft built to carry passengers; the company that operates the plane is called an airline.

The **cockpit** is a compartment in the front of an airplane where the pilot sits.

Composite materials are clothlike fibers of glass or a similar substance made rigid with special glue.

An **engineer** is a scientist trained to understand forces that act on objects such as airplanes.

Gliders are engine-less aircraft that are towed aloft by an airplane or launched from a hilltop.

Horsepower is a measurement of the speed at which an engine does work. A 1.0 horsepower engine can lift 55 pounds (25 kg) to a height of 10 feet (3 m) in one second.

An **internal combustion engine** burns fuel that drives a solid disk called a piston back and forth inside a cylinder.

Jumbo jets are big aircraft, such as a Boeing 747, that carry 400 or more passengers.

Pontoons are small, boat-like floats that serve as the landing gear of a seaplane.

A **rocket engine** is an engine that carries its own oxygen; aircraft with rocket engines can fly high in the atmosphere.

A **seaplane** is a plane that can float and is built to take off and land on water.

The **sound barrier** is the change in how an airplane flies as it approaches the speed of sound.

A speed greater than that of sound is called **supersonic**; a speed slower than sound is called subsonic.

An **ultralight** is a lightweight aircraft flown for fun; it weighs about 250 pounds (113 kg) and usually carries one person.

Index